From Pain to Purpose

A 21-Day Dedication to Living a Life
With No Excuses

Jesse S.Gines

Table of Contents

Foreword

My husband, Jesse, has an extraordinary life story that when heard, may seem very fantastical to some or unbearably familiar to others. It's an account of a lifelong struggle with pain, loss, hope, and deliverance. Much of which he had no fault in, at first, because it was created by the poor choices and circumstances of others who had authority over his life.

These early struggles then paved the way for certain mindsets to develop and mannerisms to evolve. Which in turn enabled him to continue the patterns of self-destruction in his early adult years by choosing to side with poor decision making—whether consciously or unconsciously. This book is filled with his life stories and how he was able to overcome each individual hardship. Jesse provides you with personal anecdotes that were specifically chosen to compel his readers (you) to connect with him. So that you can use it as a parameter in which self-reflection can occur, and personal growth can develop. You will also find extra challenges that require you to drive into a deeper understanding of yourself, of how you came into your circumstances, and how you can prevent them from recurring. You will find that everything within these pages is directed towards your self-talk and how you can develop a positive outlook on life through what you have experienced in your own struggles. Know that you are fully capable of controlling yourself and what choices you make, no matter what situation(s) you may find yourself in. It is all about how you retrain the way you think, and Jesse will surely guide you through this process of development.

"True change is possible when a person commits to push through adversity and allows growth to occur. Believe in yourself and be open to correct past mistakes so that your future can evolve into something much more than what it is today."
— Brenda L. Gines

Introduction

This book is more than stories—it's a journey. It's not about where I've been, but about where God can take you. For 21 days, you will walk through my life—the cracks in my foundation, the chaos of my youth, the cycles of failure, the losses, the rebuilding, the breakthroughs, and the victories. You'll see the pain I endured, but more importantly, you'll see the purpose God pulled from it. Why 21 days? Because 21 days can change your life. Research shows that habits can form in that span of time, but I believe transformation goes deeper. In 21 days, with no excuses, you can create discipline, break cycles, and start walking in freedom. This isn't just a book to read—it's a book to live. Each day gives you lessons to learn, questions to reflect on, and a "No Excuses" challenge to act on. Because change doesn't come from inspiration alone—it comes from action. My story isn't perfect, but it's real. And if God could take a broken kid from the streets, the projects, and the prisons—and turn him into a husband, father, businessman, minister, and chain-breaker— then He can do the same for you. So I invite you to lean in. Don't just skim the pages. Engage them. Wrestle with the questions. Take on the challenges. Make these 21 days a turning point in your life. At the end of this journey, my prayer is that you'll discover what I discovered: that your pain can become your purpose, and that with God, there are no excuses—only possibilities.

— Jesse S. Gines

Day 1
Valley Stream Beginnings
(Elmont Foundations)

I was born in Valley Stream, New York—but my first home was in Elmont, Long Island. 44 Seville Street was my grandparents' house. We lived in one of their upstairs apartments.

To some, Elmont might have looked ordinary. Small houses, quiet blocks, neighbors cutting their grass in the summer. But for me, it wasn't about the scenery. It was about the foundation—or more honestly, the cracks in it.
My father worked as a Correctional Officer at Rikers Island. Every day he walked into one of the toughest prisons in America, surrounded by men who had lost their freedom. His world was made of cold steel doors, echoing hallways, and hardened faces.

My mother's world was the complete opposite. She sang in the Brooklyn Tabernacle Choir, her voice carried by music that lifted hearts toward heaven.

Bars and brokenness on one side. Worship and hope on the other. It was as if God was already showing me the tension of life—the constant pull between darkness and light, bondage and freedom.

But soon after I was born, my parents separated. My father went one way. My mother shouldered the weight of raising me and my brother alone. That's how life began for me—not with stability, but with instability.

And maybe that's where you're starting too. Maybe your foundation wasn't as solid as you hoped. Maybe you didn't see the example of a full family at the table. Maybe your "home" didn't feel much like home at all.

Here's what I need you to hear: your beginning doesn't disqualify you. It prepares you.

I don't really remember my beginning—I was just a baby then. But I could feel the tension in the air. You don't get to choose where or when you are born, but you do have a say in how you finish.

Day 1 – Lessons

- You don't choose how your story begins, but you can choose how it unfolds.
- Instability may shake your house, but it doesn't have to shake your spirit.
- A cracked foundation can still hold the weight of greatness.

Day 1 - Reflection Questions

1. What "cracks" in your foundation stand out from your early years?

   _____

   _____

   _____

2. Do you see ways that God may have planted seeds of resilience in you even back then?

   _____

   _____

   _____

3. How might your instability actually have prepared you for strength later?

   _____

   _____

   _____

Day 1 - No Excuses Challenge

Write down one negative from your upbringing that you've carried as a weight. Today, flip it. Write down how that same thing has—or could—make you stronger. No excuses.

Day 2
Brooklyn Hardships
(When Safety Is Stolen)

After Elmont, life shifted again. My mother, my brother, and I moved to Southwest Brooklyn. To many, Brooklyn meant opportunity. But for us, it meant survival.

The neighborhood was alive, but not always in the ways you'd want. Kids played ball in the street, but you could also hear the sounds of sirens and arguments bleeding through thin apartment walls. Poverty wasn't distant—it was daily.
My mother tried her best, but the weight of raising us alone was heavy. Just as we thought we were finding some rhythm, life reminded us how fragile everything was.

After separating from my father, my mother decided to cohabit with another woman. At just three years old, I couldn't process what I was seeing. It was confusing to watch my mother kiss another woman.

Together, they began selling drugs to make ends meet, chasing survival in their own way. Unfortunately, this attracted all the wrong attention from all the wrong people. They made a lot of money, but strange people were always coming in and out of what we called home.

Her partner—who was always introduced to others as my mother's "sister"—became like an aunt to me. Over time, she even felt like a second mom, something of a father figure in my young eyes.

This further distorted my view of what a traditional family unit was supposed to look like. What was "normal" for others became blurry for me, leaving me with more questions than answers.

Looking back, I can see how the enemy tries to use confusion in our families to plant seeds of doubt in our hearts. But I also know that God's design for family is perfect, even if ours was broken. The Bible says, "God sets the lonely in families" (Psalm 68:6).

I didn't fully understand that at the time, but I've learned that no matter how distorted or fractured our beginnings may be, God has a way of redeeming and restoring what was lost. What felt like chaos then would one day become part of the testimony that pointed me to His order and His truth.

Selling drugs brought both money and danger. That attention drew in bad company. One night, our home was burglarized. I was just a kid, but I'll never forget the feeling. Fear walked right in through the door. It wasn't just about things being stolen—it was about safety being stolen.

For a child, the place you're supposed to feel secure became the very place you felt most vulnerable. That was Brooklyn for me. Lessons written not in textbooks, but in fear and survival.

But here's what Brooklyn taught me—and what I want you to take in: in this world there will be trouble, but we all have the ability to overcome it. Life goes on, and for many of us, we live and learn.

Day 2 – Lessons

- Life isn't fair, but God is faithful.
- Fear may knock, but faith decides who gets to stay.
- Your environment may shake you, but it doesn't have to shape you.

Day 2 - Reflection Questions

1. What "burglary" moment have you faced, when life stole your sense of security??

_____

_____

_____

2. Did it leave you more fearful—or did it force you to grow stronger?

_____

_____

_____

3. What does God's promise of strength in Isaiah 41:10 mean for your story today?

_____

_____

_____

Day 2 - No Excuses Challenge

Write down one fear that has been holding you back. Then, next to it, write one step of faith you can take today to confront it. No excuses—fear doesn't get the last word.

Day 3
Torres De Sabana
(Resilience in the Midst of Violence)

After our home was burglarized, my mother decided Brooklyn wasn't the place for us anymore. The fear that walked in through our door that night never really left. She wanted a fresh start, and in her mind, Puerto Rico seemed like it could be the answer.

We packed up whatever little was left and boarded a plane. At first, it almost felt like paradise. We stayed with family near the Yunque rainforest, surrounded by lush green trees, mountain air, and the sounds of waterfalls. For a moment, it felt like maybe this was our chance to breathe again.

But peace was short-lived. When my mother finally got us a place of our own, it wasn't in paradise. It was in Torres De Sabana—one of the most dangerous housing projects on the island.

The walls there carried echoes of gunfire. The stairwells reeked of smoke. Gangs claimed the corners, and drugs were everywhere you looked. At night, the sounds of chaos— shouting, sirens, sometimes even shots—pierced through the thin walls and made it hard to sleep.

Trust was rare. Everyone seemed to have a malicious motive. As a child, you don't always understand the depth of danger, but you feel it. I felt it walking to school, scanning my surroundings every block. I felt it lying in bed, wondering if tonight's shots would be followed by screams. I felt it watching people lose their lives to the streets.

Torres De Sabana wanted to crush me—but God was forming me. In the middle of the chaos, He was shaping a toughness inside me that no environment could steal.

This is where I want you to lean in. You may not be in a housing project, but maybe you're stuck in your own Torres De Sabana. Maybe it's a toxic workplace, a broken relationship, or a circle of people that's pulling you down. I want you to hear this: your environment doesn't have to dictate your destiny.

Puerto Rico also gave me something valuable: identity. We spoke English at home, but I was forced to learn Spanish everywhere else. I struggled at first, but little by little, I picked it up. I learned the language of my ancestors, and with it came a deeper understanding of my culture and my heritage.

More than that, I learned how to read people, how to sense what was behind their words. Even in a place surrounded by violence and dysfunction, God was giving me tools. He was building resilience, awareness, and identity.

The streets tried to break me, but instead, I walked away sharper, tougher, and more prepared for what was ahead.

So let me tell you this: no matter where you are or what situation you're facing, there is always something positive you can learn from it. Even the hardest places can become training grounds for your destiny.

Day 3 – Lessons

- Where you are doesn't define who you are.
- Chaos around you doesn't have to mean chaos within you.
- The darker the environment, the brighter God's light shines in you.

Day 3 – Reflection Questions

1. What's the "environment" in your life right now that feels crushing?

   _____

   _____

   _____

2. Do you believe God can use it to form strength in you?

   _____

   _____

   _____

3. How can you guard your spirit so your environment doesn't control your identity?

   _____

   _____

   _____

Day 3 - No Excuses Challenge

Today, list three ways you can bring peace into your environment—no matter how chaotic it is. Pray over each one, and put at least one into action. No excuses.

Day 4
Homelessness & Faith's Spark
(God's Presence in the Wilderness)

Unfortunately, Torres wasn't the end of the struggle. In fact, our financial situation grew even worse. My mother fought hard, but the money simply wasn't enough. She was trying to support two children and a drug habit at the same time, and the weight of it crushed her. Soon we hit rock bottom and became homeless.

My brother moved back to Elmont to live with our grandparents, but I couldn't bear to leave my mom. Something inside me felt responsible for her. I felt like I had to watch over her, to keep her safe, even though I was still just a kid myself. And looking back, I believe the Lord used my decision to stay to help keep her from completely falling apart.

It's one thing to struggle—it's another to not even know where you'll sleep at night. Sometimes we stayed with family. Sometimes with friends. And sometimes, we had no choice but to sleep wherever we could find a spot. But for me, none of that mattered. Home wasn't about a roof or four walls. Home was wherever my mom was, and I was willing to walk through the fire with her.

Homelessness strips you down to the core. You don't just lose comfort—you lose stability, identity, and the sense of safety every child longs for. And when you're young, that kind of instability shakes you deeply. Yet, even in those unsafe places, I now see how the Lord kept us safe. In the middle of instability, He was my stability.

And here's the truth: what was meant to break me planted a spark inside me. That spark grew into the realization that survival was never about what I held in my hands—it was about the One who had His hand on me.

The Bible says in Psalm 34:18: "The Lord is close to the brokenhearted and saves those who are crushed in spirit." I've lived that verse. Looking back, I can say with confidence—He was close. He was holding us when we couldn't hold ourselves. Maybe that's your season right now. Maybe you feel stripped of stability—financially, emotionally, relationally. Maybe you've lost things that mattered, or the bottom has fallen out of your plans.

If that's you, I want you to hear me: your lack does not mean God has left you. Your lack may be the very place He is preparing to show you His strength.

Day 4 – Lessons

- You can lose possessions, but you don't have to lose purpose.
- Stability in this world is fragile, but stability in God is unshakable.
- The lowest seasons can become the soil where faith grows the deepest.

Day 4 - Reflection Questions

1. Have you faced a season where you felt "homeless" in spirit—without direction or stability?

   _____

   _____

   _____

2. How did that season shape the way you see God as your protector and provider?

   _____

   _____

   _____

3. What area of instability must you surrender to God?

   _____

   _____

   _____

Day 4 - No Excuses Challenge

Today, take one area of instability you've been carrying—whether financial, emotional, or spiritual—and surrender it in prayer. Write it down, then underneath it write: "This is not my end. This is my training ground." Fill the page with notes, reminders, and declarations of faith that you will hold onto in the middle of instability. No excuses.

Day 5
Returning Stateside
(Elmont with My Grandparents)

When I left Puerto Rico, it wasn't because my mother had everything under control. The truth is harder to swallow. My mother was struggling—so much so that my grandparents had to step in. They gave my brother and me a home when she couldn't, because drugs had stolen her ability to care for us.

I ended up back in Elmont, Long Island—not with my mom this time, but with my grandparents. My grandfather was a construction boss in the union, working on some of Manhattan's biggest buildings like the World Trade Center, Battery Park, and Trump Tower. He woke up at 4 a.m. every morning and got home at 5:30 p.m.

My grandmother was a homemaker and a landlord. She tended to the house and rented out three apartments she had upstairs from our home on Seville Street. My brother and I shared the basement. We woke up every day at 6 a.m. for breakfast and went to sleep every night at 9 p.m. sharp.

There was no room for laziness or excuses. It was a far cry from what I was used to living on the streets with Mom, and very difficult. Structure was the key word in this house, and discipline was the theme. Their home became our new foundation.

And while I loved them for stepping in, nothing about it erased the ache inside. The truth is, my grandparents were great parents, but they weren't my parents. I missed out on a father I didn't know and a mother that wasn't there.

There's a wound that comes with watching the person who gave you life slip into addiction. Why wasn't I enough for her to stay clean? Why did I have to grow up without my mom the way I needed her? Why did life feel like it was always stacked against me?

Those questions haunted me, even as I tried to move forward. My grandparents gave us stability, but deep down, I felt the weight of abandonment.

And maybe that's your story too. Maybe someone you depended on couldn't carry the weight. Maybe you were left behind by someone you loved. If that's you, hear this: God will never leave you. What others walked away from, He steps into. Deuteronomy 31:6 says, "Be strong and courageous… for the Lord your God goes with you; he will never leave you nor forsake you."

Day 5 – Lessons

- Your story may be marked by abandonment, but it doesn't have to end in bitterness.
- What feels like rejection may actually be redirection.
- Even when parents fail, God provides others to stand in the gap.

Day 5 - Reflection Questions

1. Has someone close to you ever let you down in a way that left deep wounds?

_____

_____

_____

2. How did that abandonment shape the way you saw yourself?

_____

_____

_____

3. What area of instability must you surrender to God?

_____

_____

_____

Day 5 – No Excuses Challenge

Write down the name of one person who hurt you by leaving or failing you.

Then write these words over it: "They may have left me, but God never will."

No excuses—choose to trust the One who never abandons.

Day 6
Hustle & Grit
(The Wrong Way First)

Growing up with so much instability did something inside of me—it planted a crooked seed. It made me believe the lie that survival justified anything. If you wanted something, you got it however you could.

Unfortunately, my grandparents came from a generation where those same rules seemed to apply, and they raised me to believe that this way of life was permissible. To them, "making it" often meant bending the rules. That mindset was passed down like an heirloom, and it shaped me before I even knew what truth really was.

We went to St. Boniface Catholic Church on Sundays, but from Monday through Saturday we lived like the devil. The rituals were there—the prayers, the kneeling, the holy water—but the transformation wasn't. The moment church was over, it was back to business as usual.

Foul language wasn't just occasional—it was the native tongue in our house. Deception was applauded. If I managed to get over on someone, that meant I was clever. If I got what I wanted, even if it was dishonest, I was told I had done a good job. As long as the harm didn't touch family, it was fair game.

That was the unspoken rule, and I learned it well. I hustled, yes—but not in honorable ways. I thought stealing was normal. I thought scheming was smart. I thought cutting corners was the secret to getting ahead. At the time, it didn't feel wrong—it felt necessary, like the only option for someone trying to claw their way out of nothing.

But the truth is this: that kind of life doesn't build you up, it tears you down. It eats at your soul one compromise at a time. Broken trust. Broken friendships. Broken peace. That's what my hustle really bought me. It didn't make me strong—it made me lonely. It left me looking over my shoulder, waiting for the collapse that was sure to come.

Here's what I had to learn the hard way: just because something works in the short term doesn't mean it's right in the long term. Nothing gained dishonestly will ever stand the test of time.

Maybe you've been there too—cutting corners, lying, scheming, just to make it another day. Maybe you told yourself it was survival. But listen—what you think is survival in the moment is often just another shovel full of dirt in the hole you're digging. God's Word makes it plain. Matthew 6:33 says, "But seek first the kingdom of God and his righteousness, and all these things will be given to you as well."

That means we don't have to scheme. We don't have to steal. We don't have to compromise. If we seek Him first, He provides. His way may take longer, it may feel harder, it may test your patience, but unlike the hustle—it lasts.

Day 6 – Lessons from My Wrong Hustle

- Dishonorable shortcuts lead to dead ends.
- What you build dishonestly will eventually collapse.
- God's way may take long but it lasts forever.

Day 6 - Reflection Questions

1. Have you ever tried to hustle your way into survival the wrong way?

_____

_____

_____

2. What did it cost you in the long run—peace, friendships, integrity?

_____

_____

_____

3. Do you believe Matthew 6:33—that God will provide if you put Him first?

_____

_____

_____

Day 6 – No Excuses Challenge

Think of one area where you've been tempted to cut corners or compromise. Write it down, then underneath, write:

"I will seek God's kingdom first. He will provide."

No excuses—commit to doing it God's way.

Day 7
Meeting My Father & New Life For Youth

After years of instability, I finally came face to face with someone I had mostly known from a distance: my father. By then, he wasn't the same man who had walked away years earlier. Alcoholism had nearly destroyed him—chewed him up, spit him out, and left him at rock bottom. But God got ahold of him. He was delivered, redeemed, and when I met him again, he stood as the Assistant Director of New Life For Youth, a Christian men's drug and alcohol treatment center tucked away in Beaverdam, Virginia.

When my brother and I moved into the facility with him, it felt like stepping into another world. In many ways, it was a breath of fresh air after years of suffocating pain. I admired my father deeply. For the first time, I saw him as a man who preached the gospel, prayed with the broken, and walked alongside men who were clawing their way out of addiction. He wasn't perfect, but to me, he was everything I needed in a father at that moment. I watched him stand tall where once he had fallen flat, and it gave me hope that God could rewrite even the darkest chapters.

Yet, as beautiful as that transformation was, "the Ranch" came with its own challenges. Though he was our father, he was also a stranger to the daily work of raising children—especially children scarred by years of abandonment and suffering. We were trying to learn him, and he was trying to learn us. I had already endured twelve years of pain, betrayal, and instability; trust didn't come easily.

Ranch life was odd—holy on one hand, chaotic on the other. Imagine being a kid surrounded by men fresh out of jail, men who bore the marks of the streets and the weight of their past. It wasn't the typical environment to grow up in. Most kids my age were surrounded by classmates, toys, and neighborhood games. I was surrounded by testimonies—men in the process of being rebuilt by the hand of God. In a strange way, it was perfect for me. I had seen instability my whole life, and now I was living in a place designed to restore it.

But not everything was easy. At school, I faced racism and rejection. People saw our skin color, our faith, and our background, and they decided we didn't belong. I was bullied, mocked, and made to feel like an outsider. And though I had always been a fighter, something in me had changed. My newfound faith in Jesus Christ whispered to me that I didn't have to swing every time someone swung at me. Turning the other cheek wasn't weakness—it was obedience. Still, it was hard. Real hard. Every insult, every shove, every smirk tested me.

But rejection taught me something valuable: rejection is often just confirmation that you're set apart for something greater. Living at New Life For Youth was more than an experience—it was a revelation. I saw my father rise from the ashes of addiction into leadership. I saw broken men rediscover their dignity, their faith, and their families. And I learned firsthand that the world's rejection can never override God's acceptance.

John 15:18 reminded me then (and reminds me now): "If the world hates you, keep in mind that it hated me first." That season taught me that God doesn't just heal individuals—He restores families.

Day 7 – Lessons from New Life For Youth

- God can rewrite anyone's story.
- Your identity isn't in peoples approval, it's in Christ.
- Rejection from the world can actually be God's protection

Day 7 – Reflection Questions

1. Who in your life has God restored when you thought they were too far gone?

   _____

   _____

   _____

2. Have you ever faced rejection because of your faith or identity? How did it shape you?

   _____

   _____

   _____

3. Where are you still seeking the approval of people more than God?

   _____

   _____

   _____

Day 7 - No Excuses Challenge

Write down one rejection you've faced that still stings.

Underneath it, write:

"This does not define me. My identity is in Christ."

No excuses—root your worth in Him.

Day 8
The Bronx, Gangs, and My First Jail Cell

After New Life, my father tried to start a new program in the Bronx. Hope pulled us north, toward the city that never sleeps — the city people called the land of opportunity, but for me it became a classroom of pain. We packed up what little we had and headed out to the big city of dreams.

We settled in a storefront on Webster Avenue, not far from Fordham Road and the Bronx Zoo. To a kid, it felt like we had been dropped right into the center of the world. Noise everywhere. Subways rumbling beneath the streets. Sirens screaming through the night. Life in the Bronx was fast, loud, and relentless.

While my father was busy working on launching his program, my brother and I were busy doing the opposite—terrorizing the neighborhood. At just 14 years old, my mind was consumed with two things: girls and fitting in. I didn't care about ministry, structure, or school. I cared about respect. I cared about belonging.

But the new rehab didn't last long. The fire marshal shut it down, and just like that, our fragile hopes collapsed. We moved again, this time into the Allerton Avenue Co-Ops on Bronx Park East— one of the most notorious projects in the city.

Life grew heavier that summer. My grandmother—my father's mother—passed away, and the grief cut deep. Not long after, my father remarried. Trying to rebuild his life, he landed a job as head of security at the World Trade Center. To outsiders, it looked like stability was finally coming together. But at home, his schedule created another void.

Dad worked nights, leaving the house around 1 p.m. and returning at 3 in the morning. Exhaustion kept him in bed until late morning the next day. That meant my brother and I were left to ourselves most nights. And left alone, we made our own rules. We skipped school, cut corners, and let the streets become our teachers.

The Bloods became our family. Gangs promised respect. Drugs promised belonging. But those promises were lies that only forged chains. The need to be accepted blinded me. What I thought was loyalty was really bondage. What I thought was belonging was really destruction. And before long, those chains dragged me straight into addiction, rebellion, and consequences I couldn't escape.

It didn't take long before those choices landed me in my first jail cell. Spofford, a juvenile detention center, was where I found myself. I'll never forget the shock of it—the cold steel against my skin, the echo of slamming doors, the emptiness of a cage meant for broken kids.

And sitting there, it hit me: it wasn't just my environment that put me there—it was my decisions. Galatians 6:7 says, "Do not be deceived: God cannot be mocked. A man reaps what he sows." That verse became real to me. I had sown recklessness, rebellion, and compromise. And now I was reaping pain, loneliness, and regret.

But even in that cell, I felt something greater than punishment—I felt a seed of hope being planted. God was already beginning to write a different chapter.

Day 8 – Lessons

- The need for acceptance can lead you into bondage.
- What feels like belonging is usually a trap.
- Every choice has a cost. You can't outrun consequesnces.

Day 8 - Reflection Questions

1. Have you ever compromised who you are just to fit in? What did it cost you?

_____

_____

_____

2. Who or what has been your "gang"—the crowd, habit, or influence that tried to own your identity?

_____

_____

_____

3. Can you admit where your own choices, not just circumstances, led to consequences?

_____

_____

_____

Day 8 – No Excuses Challenge

Write down one area where you've been tempted to "fit in" at the cost of your identity. Under it, write:

"I will not be owned by acceptance. I belong to God."

No excuses—choose belonging in Christ over the crowd.

Day 9
Jail, Cycles, and the Hardest Lessons

The Bronx set me on a path I couldn't easily escape. My first real taste of the system came at Spofford Juvenile Detention Center. Spofford wasn't built to rehabilitate—it was built to contain. Cold walls, sharp voices, and broken souls surrounded me. For some kids, this was routine—a revolving door they walked through again and again. For me, it was my first time, and I made a vow to myself: I would never come back.

But vows made in fear are fragile. From Spofford, I was sentenced to a military-style boot camp in Columbia, South Carolina, called Midlands Evaluation Center. It was strict, harsh, relentless. Drills at dawn. Push-ups until your arms shook. Voices barking orders until your ears rang.

For a while, I thought maybe this could change me. Maybe fear, discipline, and pain would break the cycle. But here's the truth: you can change someone's environment, but if their heart doesn't change, the cycle continues. And my heart hadn't yet been surrendered.

I was released with five years of probation. It sounded like freedom, but probation only works if you leave behind the life that put you there. I didn't. The streets still called my name, and I answered. That promise I made at Spofford to never return? I broke it quickly. I violated probation and landed in adult jail.

I was released, then re-arrested. I'll never forget one Christmas Eve—I was released in the morning and back behind bars by nightfall, arrested on a new charge. The cycle became my life. Released. Arrested. Released. Arrested again. Felony after felony. Each time, I told myself I'd change. Each time, I couldn't. Crime and addiction had their grip on me, and the next five years blurred into steel bars, broken promises, and the hollow echo of my own failures.

I had created my own wilderness—wandering in circles, never moving forward, never finding peace. And every time, the same lesson stared me in the face: I couldn't do it on my own. Only God could break the cycle. Only His discipline could produce real change. Hebrews 12:11 says, "No discipline seems pleasant at the time, but painful. Later on, however, it produces a harvest of righteousness and peace for those who have been trained by it."

The more I resisted, the more painful it became. But God was training me. Every cell, every consequence, every sleepless night behind bars was chiseling away at my pride.

The five-plus years I spent behind bars were some of the worst years of my life. I'll never forget them. I'll never forget the lessons. And I wouldn't wish that cycle on my worst enemy. But those years also became the soil where God began planting something new.

Day 9 – Lessons

- Environment can restrain you, but only God can transform you.
- You can't put-hustle consequences.
- Cycles end only through surrender.

Day 9 - Reflection Questions

1. What "cycle" have you repeated in your life?

_____

_____

_____

2. How have consequences taught you more than comfort ever could?

_____

_____

_____

3. Do you believe surrender is stronger than willpower?

_____

_____

_____

Day 9 - No Excuses Challenge

Write down one destructive cycle you keep falling back into.

Instead of saying "I'll fix it," write:

"God, I surrender this to You."

Take one obedient step today—no excuses.

Day 10
The Best and Worst Year (2005)

Then came the year that changed everything: 2005. It was the year I felt the deepest pain and the greatest joy.

Soon after my final sentence, I reunited with my mother. By this time, she was clean and working on mending her life back together again. My brother had also gotten out of the penitentiary on five years of parole. My grandfather bought my mother a house in beautiful St. Cloud, Florida—an up-and-coming town near Disney World.

I had a girlfriend, and for a while, life was good again. I completed my probation, started attending

Freedom Tabernacle Church in Kissimmee, Florida, and even

found my own place to live. I began planning a wedding with

my girlfriend at the time.

But my brother—my blood, my partner in crime, the one who walked the same streets with me—never chose to leave that life. He visited the church a couple of times, but crime seemed more attractive to him in those days. His refusal to give up that life cost him everything.

I'll never forget the day I lost him. Death is final. It rips away illusions. It reminds you that sin leads to destruction, and tomorrow is never guaranteed. This was the worst pain I had ever experienced, and I knew it would never go away.

And yet, in that same year, I also became a husband. Shortly after, I became a father. I held my first child in my arms, feeling the weight of responsibility and the joy of new life while still carrying the pain of a recent death.

How could one year hold so much pain and so much blessing? How could I bury my brother and cradle my child in the same season?

2005 taught me this: life and death often run side by side. The choices we make determine which one will define us. On one hand, I saw the cost of destruction. On the other, I saw the promise of legacy.

Deuteronomy 30:19 says, "I have set before you life and death, blessings and curses. Now choose life, so that you and your children may live." That year, I realized my choices weren't just about me anymore. They were about my family—about whether I would repeat the cycle, or break it.

Day 10 – Lessons

- Life and death often run side by side.
- Your choices don't just affect you, they affect your legacy.
- Choosing life means choosing your family, not just yourself.

Day 10 – Reflection Questions

1. Have you ever had a year where joy and pain collided?

   _____

   _____

   _____

2. What losses remind you of the danger of living outside God's will?

   _____

   _____

   _____

3. What blessings remind you why it's worth choosing Him?

   _____

   _____

   _____

Day 10 - No Excuses Challenge

Make two lists: "What destruction has cost me" and "What blessings God has given me."

Look at them side by side and declare:

"I choose life—for me and my family."

Day 11
Marriage, Betrayal, and Loneliness

After 2005, I was determined to live as a husband and father. I owed it to my brother's memory, I owed it to my parents, I owed it to myself—but most of all, I owed it to my children. I wanted to give them the stability and love I never had. I promised myself I would be the man my family could lean on.

But here's the truth: marriage takes two people walking in the same direction. Two people who share the same vision, the same sacrifice, the same commitment. No matter how hard I tried, my wife didn't seem to want to be a wife or a mother. After the birth of our second child, the cracks grew wider. And the pain didn't come from outside my home—it came from within it.

I was faithful to God, a good husband, a present father, and a provider who worked daily to support my family. But my wife carried a troubled upbringing of her own. Her boredom with the quiet life of being a housewife, coupled with her own fleshly desires, pushed her to seek "more" outside of our marriage.

She cheated on me—not once, but repeatedly. Each betrayal was like a dagger that went deeper than the last. And then came the moment that crushed me: in the middle of her unfaithfulness, she became pregnant—and chose to abort the child. That life could have been my third child. A son or daughter I would never know.

No matter how much I prayed, worked, forgave, and tried to hold the marriage together, I couldn't make her be faithful. Eventually, we split. For six months, I lived in a cold, empty house—without my children. Silence filled the rooms where their laughter used to echo. I'd walk through the house and feel the weight of absence pressing against the walls.
That's when I learned one of the hardest truths of life: you cannot force someone to be who they refuse to be.

But I also discovered this: even when people betray you, God never will. Even when a house feels empty, His presence fills it. Even when you feel abandoned, you are never alone. Psalm 27:10 became my anchor: "Though my father and mother forsake me, the Lord will receive me." The same applies to spouses, friends, or anyone else. They may walk away—but God never does..

Day 11 – Lessons from Marriage, Betrayal, and Loneliness

- You cannot force someone to be who they refuse to be.
- Even when people betray you God never will.
- Loneliness may surround you but God's presence will fill you.

Day 11 - Reflection Questions

1. Have you faced betrayal from someone you loved?

_____

_____

_____

2. How did that season change your trust in people?

_____

_____

_____

3. Where has God shown you His presence in loneliness?

_____

_____

_____

Day 11 – No Excuses Challenge

Write down one wound from betrayal you've carried too long. Place your hand over it and say:

"I release this to God. I will not let betrayal define me. I will let His faithfulness refine me."

No excuses—choose healing.

Day 12
The Redemption of the Father

In the middle of heartbreak, I turned to prayer. Every night, I lifted my children before God's throne. I prayed that He would restore what I couldn't repair. I prayed that He would return what the enemy had stolen from me.

I remember driving to my church when the doors weren't even open, just parking in the lot and weeping alone. One of those days, my pastor and his wife showed up unexpectedly. He didn't just offer small talk—he sat with me in the brokenness. We prayed together. I poured out my pain, my confusion, my anger, and my longing. I'll never forget what he said:

"Jesse, I can't promise that God will bring your wife and kids back, but I can promise you that the Lord will bless you with someone ten times better than what the enemy stole."

At the time, those words didn't comfort me. I didn't want "better." I wanted what I thought was normal—going to work, coming home to my wife and kids, even if the ache of betrayal haunted me. I thought every man lived with that shadow of doubt. I thought compromise was part of the package.

But God had another plan. His timing is never rushed, never

delayed—it arrives exactly when our hearts are ready. One day, completely out of the blue, my ex-wife dropped by and handed me my children. She told me she'd be back in a few days, but the truth is—she never came back. Just like that, I became a single father.

It wasn't easy. Fatherhood already carries a weight; single fatherhood can feel crushing. But I was grateful. I was thankful. And I quickly discovered this: when your strength runs out, God's strength begins. Being a single dad forced me into deeper dependence on God. I leaned on Him for provision, for wisdom, for patience, and for love. And each time I cried out, He showed up.

And then, in His perfect timing, God surprised me with something I never expected. He rekindled a long-lost relationship with my high school sweetheart. After all those years, we found each other again. This time, the love was stronger, deeper, more rooted in faith. I asked her to marry me, and she said yes.

But it didn't stop there. She didn't just marry me—she became a mother to my children. She chose them, adopted them, and loved them as if she had birthed them herself. That is redemption. That is God's signature—taking broken pieces and crafting something beautiful out of them.

Joel 2:25 says, "I will restore to you the years that the locust has eaten..." That wasn't just a verse on a page—it became my life. God restored. God rebuilt. God redeemed.

Day 12 – Lessons from The Redemption of the Father

- God redeems what we cannot fix.
- Difficulties you face become a testimony of God's strength .
- Redemption often comes through people God sends into your life.

Day 12 - Reflection Questions

1. Have you ever prayed for something that seemed impossible? How did God answer?

_____

_____

_____

2. How has God shown Himself as a Father to you?

_____

_____

_____

3. Who has He brought into your life to redeem what others broke?

_____

_____

_____

Day 12 - No Excuses Challenge

Write down one area that feels beyond repair. Next to it, write:

"God is my Redeemer. He can restore this too."

Pray over it today. No excuses—trust Him fully.

Day 13
From Survival to Influence

When God restored my family, I realized it was more than a gift for me—it was a calling. He wasn't just piecing my life back together. He was preparing me to influence others. He was turning my pain into purpose.

But here's what I've learned: influence never comes without fire. Just as diamonds are formed under pressure, influence is forged in trials. Survival teaches you how to make it through. Influence requires building something that lasts—and anything that lasts will be tested.

Too many people buy into a false narrative about salvation. They think giving your life to God means everything just works out—that bags of money fall from the sky, that spouses come running back, that life floats along in effortless bliss. But that's not the gospel of Scripture. That's fantasy.

The Bible shows us a different picture: one of fire, battles, prison bars, and perseverance. Yes, Romans 8:28 promises, "And we know that in all things God works for the good of those who love him, who have been called according to his purpose." But we forget that "all things" often include pain, disappointment, and loss. Look at the examples. Joseph dreamed of greatness, yet was betrayed by his brothers, sold into slavery, and falsely accused before God exalted him to second-in-command in Egypt. David was anointed king but spent years running from Saul, hiding in caves before he ever sat on a throne. Job lost everything he had, yet his faith gave him double in the end. Daniel was thrown into the lions' den. His closest friends were cast into the fiery furnace. And yet, in every story, God was in the fire with them. None of them reached their promise without pain. None of them walked into destiny without fire.

My own life followed the same pattern. I stepped into new arenas—business, ministry, and fitness. Business wasn't just about money. It became proof that faith, discipline, and integrity create opportunities. Ministry wasn't just about preaching sermons. It was living testimony that if God could restore me, He could restore anyone. Fitness wasn't just about my body. It was about showing that discipline in the physical mirrors discipline in the spiritual (and trust me, that's another book on its own). But the testing never stopped. Just when I thought I was standing strong, one of the greatest trials hit: our home burned down. In a single moment, years of hard work turned into ashes. I could have quit. I could have asked, "Why me?" Instead, God reminded me of Job—who, in the ashes of his life, declared, "Though He slay me, yet will I trust Him."

And I did. I believed that if God could restore my family, He could restore my home. If He gave me the vision for business, He could give me the strength to rebuild. And so, we pressed on. We prayed. We persevered. And we saw His faithfulness yet again. Here's the truth: influence isn't born in easy seasons. It's forged when you remain faithful through the hardest ones. James 1:12 says, "Blessed is the one who perseveres under trial because, having stood the test, that person will receive the crown of life that the Lord has promised to those who love him."

Day 13 – Lessons from From Survival to Influence

- Survival teaches grit, but influence requires faith.
- Trials don't mean you're off track, they mean you're being refined.
- When you stay faithful in the fire, God restores greater than what you lost.

Day 13 – Reflection Questions

1. Where is God calling you to move from survival into influence?

   _____

   _____

   _____

2. How have trials been testing you while you try to build?

   _____

   _____

   _____

3. Do you believe God restores greater than what was lost?

   _____

   _____

   _____

Day 13 - No Excuses Challenge

Write down one current trial you're facing. Instead of asking "Why me?" ask: "What is God building in me through this?" No excuses—choose faith over frustration.

Day 14
Leadership in the Fire

After the fire, God provided the resources to rebuild our house. But He didn't just restore it—He multiplied it. The new home was bigger, better, and stronger than the one that had burned. A home ready to hold my growing family—now five children in total.

At the same time, my business was thriving. I had earned my real estate license and built a construction-real estate hybrid company. God was blessing the work of my hands. But don't mistake blessing for ease. Every brick of progress came with sweat, setbacks, and sacrifice. I learned this truth: building is tough.

Whether it's a family, a business, or a house, it takes hard work. Late nights. Early mornings. Dedication when you'd rather rest. Sacrifice when you'd rather quit. And none of it happened overnight. I failed my real estate license exam six times before passing. At first, I sold timeshares because I couldn't afford to join the board of realtors.

It took five years of grinding in real estate before I finally got my broker's license— and even then, I failed that exam three times before I made it through.

The same was true of my house. It didn't just rise out of the ashes on its own. With the help of my friend Juan Rubio (RIP), my friend Shawn, and my uncle Billy, we built it together—sweat, grit, and all.

Growth takes time. Discipline. Dedication. Friend, I need you to hear this: nothing worth having comes easy. Leadership in the fire means carrying responsibility even when the weight feels unbearable. It's not about being perfect—it's about being faithful. It's about showing up, even when you're tired. It's about carrying the load, even when no one claps for you. And that's what God was showing me: He multiplies what you surrender to Him, but He doesn't remove the responsibility. He strengthens you to carry it.

Yes, "with great power comes great responsibility." And Scripture says the same: only when we are "faithful with little" will God entrust us with more. Matthew 6:33 became the foundation of my leadership: "But seek first his kingdom and his righteousness, and all these things will be given to you as well."

Day 14 – Lessons from Leadership in the Fire

- God doesn't just restore—He multiplies.
- Building requires hard work and dedication.
- Leadership is tested under pressure.

Day 14 - Reflection Questions

1. What are you currently building—family, career, ministry?

_____

_____

_____

2. Where has God multiplied what you surrendered?

_____

_____

_____

3. How can you be faithful in leadership, not perfect?

_____

_____

_____

Day 14 - No Excuses Challenge

Pick one area of your life you're "building." Write down three disciplines you will commit to this week to strengthen it.

No excuses—faith plus discipline builds greatness.

Day 15
Breaking Generational Chains

As my family and business grew, I began to see the bigger picture. God wasn't just blessing me—He was breaking chains through me. Chains of poverty. Chains of addiction. Chains of broken homes and instability that haunted my family line for generations.

For too long, those chains defined us. They told the story of where we came from, but not where we were going. In Christ, they ended with me. What ran in my family ran into me. And by God's power, it stopped here.

But don't get it twisted—breaking chains is never easy. Being a married man and raising five children tested me daily. Loving and providing for my wife and kids sacrificially stretched me further than I thought I could stretch. Building a business while also growing in ministry stretched me even further.

Some days I felt like I was breaking under the weight—but I realized something powerful: all the pain I went through in my past was God's weight room, preparing me to carry this load. Every season of struggle was a set. Every failure was a rep. Every tear was part of the training. And now I could handle more because I had been forged by fire. I came to understand that this journey was never just about me.

It was about others. It was about my family. It was about the people watching. It was about those who would come after me. God was teaching me to live selfless instead of selfish, to die to myself daily so others could live free. Breaking chains requires sacrifice. It requires discipline. It requires looking temptation in the face and saying: Not today. Not on my watch. Not in my bloodline. Because here's the truth: your children inherit what you practice, not what you preach. If they see you live in compromise, they will inherit compromise. But if they see you live in surrender, obedience, and faith—they inherit freedom. That is legacy. That is generational wealth—the kind that money can't buy.

Jesus said in John 16:33, "In this world you will have trouble. But take heart! I have overcome the world." And if He overcame, then so can I. In fact, He promised that through His Spirit, we would do even greater things on this earth. That means every chain the enemy tried to use to bind me has already been defeated.

Exodus 20:6 promises that God shows love "to a thousand

generations of those who love me and keep my commandments."

That's chain-breaking power. That's legacy. That's the testimony I want to leave behind—not just that I survived, but that I overcame.

When I think back to all my hardships, all my struggles, all my

pain—I wouldn't trade it for anything. If I could go back in

time,

I wouldn't change a thing. Because every scar became a story. Every bruise became a lesson. Every battle became a platform. And together, they became my legacy.

Friend, hear me: the chains in your family line may look unbreakable. But in Christ, they end with you..

Day 15 – Lessons from Breaking Generational Chains

- What ran in your family can end with you.
- Pain is God's wight room, it prepares you to carry more.
- Your children inherit what you practice, not what you preach.

Day 15 - Reflection Questions

1. What chains have followed your family line that need to stop with you?

_____

_____

_____

2. How has God used your past pain to prepare you for present responsibility?

_____

_____

_____

3. What example are you actively practicing for your children—or those who look up to you?

_____

_____

_____

Day 15 - No Excuses Challenge

Write down one generational chain you refuse to pass on. Then declare:

"This ends with me. My children will inherit freedom, not bondage.

My family will inherit faith, not fear. My bloodline belongs to Jesus."

No excuses—live it out.

Day 16
Fitness as Faith

By now, I could see it clearly: had it not been for the pain, I wouldn't be strong enough. My childhood, the betrayals, the losses, the fire—all of it had built resilience. The weight of my past was training for the weight of my present.

But there came a moment when I realized I was carrying the wrong kind of weight. One day, I stepped on the scale and nearly fell off. Two hundred and forty-five pounds. For a man who had always been active, always moving, it was shocking. I knew I was out of balance. Poor eating habits, sweets, and overeating had taken their toll. My spirit was strong, but my body was groaning under the weight of neglect.

Then came the breaking point. After church one afternoon, I was playing basketball with the teens. I went up for a flashy layup, and pop!—my patellar tendon snapped. Just like that, I was bedridden, waiting four months for surgery. And when the surgery finally came, recovery took nearly six more.

When I could finally walk again, fear crept in. Fear whispered that the same thing could happen to my other knee. Fear told me to play it safe, to stop pushing, to settle. And for a while, I listened. But fear is a liar. Fear doesn't just keep you out of the gym—it keeps you from your destiny.

Then God used a brother named Javier from my church, who invited me to a free 10-week training program. I accepted—and it changed everything. I decided to hit the gym as hard and relentlessly as I pursued the Lord. And just like that, fitness became a parallel to faith.

The gym taught me: no pain, no gain. You can't build muscle without first breaking it down. Easy come, easy go—but what's forged through struggle lasts. I began to see the gym as more than just a place for weights. It became a sanctuary. It became a church for my body. Every rep was like a prayer. Every drop of sweat was like an offering. And God answered.

The Apostle Paul put it plainly in 1 Corinthians 9:27: "But I discipline my body and bring it into subjection, lest, when I have preached to others, I myself should become disqualified." Paul knew the connection—if you can't control your body, your spirit will suffer. If you're lazy in one, you'll be lazy in the other. If you discipline one, you strengthen the other.

Fitness became more than a workout—it became worship. Each push-up was perseverance. Each set was a sermon. Each drop of sweat reminded me that discipline is the doorway to freedom.

Friend, let me tell you: when you bring your body under control, you begin to taste the freedom God promises. You prove to yourself that you can conquer flesh, that you can resist excuses, and that you can live in victory.

Fitness was never just about looking better in the mirror. It was about becoming the man God called me to be—strong in body, sharp in spirit, disciplined in every area of life. And I knew this: if I was going to preach discipline, I had to live it. If I was going to call others to transformation, I had to walk it.

God was molding me with every rep, preparing me to be a living testimony that discipline is not punishment—it's freedom.

Day 16 – Lessons from Fitness as Faith

- Pain is not punishment—it's preparation.
- Discipline in the physical realm strengthens the spiritual.
- Fitness is worship when done in surrender to God.

Day 16 – Reflection Questions

1. Where have you let fear keep you from discipline?

_____

_____

_____

2. How can you begin to treat your body as a temple and not a burden?

_____

_____

_____

3. What spiritual lessons can you draw from your physical habits?

_____

_____

_____

Day 16 - No Excuses Challenge

This week, commit to one new discipline in your fitness—whether it's a healthier meal, a daily walk, or a workout routine. Each time you feel the pain or resistance, whisper to yourself: "This is worship. This is freedom."

No excuses—let fitness build your faith.

Day 17
The "No Excuses" Philosophy

By this point, my life had proven one thing over and over again: excuses are the enemy of greatness. Excuses are weakness disguised as reason. They are laziness dressed up like logic.

They sound harmless — "I'm too tired... it's not the right time... I didn't grow up with the right opportunities" — but excuses are deadly. They keep you small, keep you stuck, and rob you of the life God created you to live.

The Bible warns us in Proverbs 24:33–34: "A little sleep, a little slumber, a little folding of the hands to rest—and poverty will come on you like a thief and scarcity like an armed man."

Excuses are a slow fade into destruction. They promise comfort, but they deliver poverty—spiritual, financial, and emotional.

I had every excuse to quit. My mother's addiction. My father's absence. The gangs. The jail time. Betrayal. A burned-down house. But excuses don't build legacies. Excuses bury them.

The flesh always looks for the easy way out. And the easiest way out is always an excuse — why you can't instead of why you can. Excuses make victims. Discipline makes victors.

Jesus spoke plainly in Luke 9:23: "Whoever wants to be my disciple must deny themselves and take up their cross daily and follow me." He didn't say make excuses. He said deny yourself.

That's why I chose long ago: no excuses. Not in family. Not in business. Not in ministry. Not in fitness. If God calls me to it, He will give me the grace to carry it. And if I stumble and fall, I'll get up again.

Listen to me, friend: you may have a past, but it is not final.

We live in a time where excuses are the norm:
- "I didn't have a father figure."
- "My wife doesn't respect me."
- "My past is too messed up."
- "I'm too busy."

But God isn't looking for excuse-makers. He's calling for fighters. He's calling for men and women who will rise above excuses and walk in strength.

So let me speak plainly:

- If you're blaming your past — it's time to let it go.

- If you're hiding behind fear , it's time to face it with faith

- If you're waiting for perfect conditions, you'll never move.

No more excuses!

You are called.

You are chosen.

You are equipped.

Now act like it.

If you're ready to believe in God without excuses — stand up.

If you're ready to lead your home, fight for your faith, and walk in holiness — the time is now.

No more compromise.

No more delay.

No more excuses!

Day 17 – Lessons from The "No Excuses" Philosophy

- Excuses keep you small; discipline makes you great.
- Your flesh seeks comfort, but your spirit is forged in challenge.
- You can't be a victim and a victor at the same time.

Day 17 - Reflection Questions

1. What excuses have been keeping you from moving forward?

_____

_____

_____

2. Do you view excuses as harmless—or as chains?

_____

_____

_____

3. Where in your life do you need to stop being a victim and start being a victor?

_____

_____

_____

Day 17 - No Excuses Challenge

Write down your top three excuses. Cross them out, and replace each with a statement of action:

"I will because God called me."

No excuses—choose victory today!

Day 18
Building Others Up

Influence doesn't start with a stage—it starts at home. Too many people dream about changing the world but neglect the very people sitting at their dinner table.

For me, influence began with a daily, non-negotiable commitment: prayer with my wife and children at 7:00 PM. That time is sacred. To this day, we keep it. Everyone who knows me knows this. We don't stay out late, we don't put anything before that time. Vacation, Airbnb, hotel—wherever we are, whatever we're doing, at 7 o'clock we drop everything and pray.

I've been doing this for over 15 years now. Why? Because my first ministry is my family. Paul wrote in 1 Timothy 5:8: "Anyone who does not provide for their relatives, and especially for their own household, has denied the faith and is worse than an unbeliever."

Provision isn't only about putting food on the table. It's about feeding the soul. It's about bringing the Word of God into the home. I am the pastor and leader of my household, and I take that call seriously. God sees that I am faithful with my family first—because if I can't lead at home, I can't lead anywhere else.

From there, God widened the circle. He began multiplying what started in my living room.

I started speaking in jails weekly, pouring into men I once related to all too well. I told them: "I've been where you are— but you don't have to stay here. Discipline and God's grace can bring you out."

Then came small church groups—rooms filled with hungry people, ready for the truth, uncut and without sugar-coating. I didn't come to entertain; I came to declare that freedom is possible through Jesus Christ.

Even in business, God gave me a platform. Leading real estate agents, I taught them integrity—doing the right thing when nobody's watching. Because success without integrity is failure in disguise. You can make millions and still be bankrupt if your character is rotten.

This is God's design: multiplication. Genesis says everything reproduces after its kind. Who you are is what you reproduce. If you're bitter, bitterness spreads. If you're disciplined, discipline spreads. If you're faithful, faith spreads.

The Parable of the Sower reminds us: the seed is always good— but the soil matters. My job was never to change the seed. My assignment was to prepare the soil of every life I touched—at home, in jail, in church, in business. Prayer softens the soil.

Integrity pulls the weeds. Consistency

guards against the birds. And when the soil is ready, the seed

multiplies. That is how influence works. Not by chasing stages,

but by

planting faithfully. Not by demanding platforms, but by

stewarding whatever ground God places in front of you. And if

you're faithful in the small, God will make you ruler over

much.

Day 18 – Lessons from Building Others Up

- True influence starts at home, not on a stage.
- Who you are is what you reproduce, integrity, faith, and discipline multiply.
- The seed is always good, but the soul must be prepared.

Day 18 - Reflection Questions

1. How are you intentionally building up your family as your first ministry?

_____

_____

_____

2. What are you reproducing in others—faith, discipline, bitterness, or compromise?

_____

_____

_____

3. Where is God calling you to prepare soil instead of chasing stages?

_____

_____

_____

Day 18 - No Excuses Challenge

Choose one area of influence—your home, your workplace, your

church, or your community. Ask yourself: "What soil am I

preparing here?"

Then commit to one daily action that builds others up with

integrity, faith, and consistency.

No excuses—be faithful where you are, and watch God multiply

it.

Day 19
Living Bold, Living Free

Freedom isn't just being released from chains—it's learning to never pick them back up.

For years, I let my past define me. Gangs. Drugs. Jail. Betrayal. Excuses. I wore those labels like prison clothes. Even after God opened the door, I still carried the weight of them around my neck.

But here's what I learned: Jesus doesn't just break chains—He reassigns your life. He doesn't just set you free—He calls you to live differently.

Living bold means refusing to shrink back into fear. Living free means refusing to return to the places, people, and patterns that once bound you.

And let me be real with you: it isn't easy. Temptations still come. Old voices still whisper. Fear still tries to creep in. Your flesh will always look for shortcuts, comfort, and excuses.

But Galatians 5:1 makes it plain: "It is for freedom that Christ has set us free. Stand firm, then, and do not let yourselves be burdened again by a yoke of slavery."

Freedom is your right as God's child. Boldness is your responsibility as His witness. But here's the question: what are you doing with your freedom?

Because freedom without discipline is just another kind of bondage. If you're free but lazy, you're still chained. If you're free but undisciplined, you'll slide right back into the pit you crawled out of.

The truth is simple: laziness robs destiny. Excuses rob purpose. A lack of discipline destroys freedom faster than sin ever will. Why? Because when you refuse discipline, you volunteer for chains.

So hear me today—if you've been coasting, if you've been waiting, if you've been living in "someday," it's time to wake up. Bold living doesn't wait for perfect conditions. Free living doesn't ask permission. You've got one life, one shot, one opportunity to live out God's calling—don't waste it.

Ask yourself these questions:

1. What good is a redeemed soul if you live like a slave to excuses?
2. What good is an open Bible if you never discipline yourself to live it out?
3. What good is potential if you bury it under procrastination?

Living bold and free means:

- Saying no to shortcuts and yes to discipline.
- Saying no to laziness and yes to responsibility.
- Saying no to fear and yes to faith.

Your family needs you bold. Your community needs you free. Your calling demands your discipline.

Friend, you're not just fighting for your own freedom—you're breaking chains for your children, your grandchildren, and every person who will come after you.

What runs in your family can end with you. Don't hand excuses to the next generation—hand them discipline, boldness, and freedom.

It's time to step up.

It's time to stand firm.

It's time to live bold.

It's time to live free.

Day 19 – Lessons from Living Bold, Living Free

- Freedom without discipline is just another kind of bondage.
- Laziness robs destiny; excuses destroy legacy.
- Boldness is not an option, it is your responsibility as God's witness.

Day 19 - Reflection Questions

1. Where in your life have you confused "freedom" with laziness or lack of discipline?

_____

_____

_____

2. What voices or patterns from your past still try to pull you back into bondage?

_____

_____

_____

3. What bold step can you take today to show your family and community what true freedom looks like?

_____

_____

_____

Day 19 - No Excuses Challenge

Write down the one area where you've been most

undisciplined—fitness, finances, faith, or family. Next to it,
write:

"I refuse chains. I choose freedom through discipline."

Then take one bold step today—don't wait until tomorrow. No

excuses

Day 20
Leaving a Legacy

Legacy isn't property, cars, or titles. Legacy is the imprint of your life on those who come after you.

For me, it began at home. I wasn't just raising children—I was breaking cycles. I wasn't just building a house—I was building a home where love, discipline, and faith ruled. My children weren't just inheriting my name; they were inheriting my example. They would either inherit excuses, or they would inherit endurance. They would either inherit bondage, or they would inherit freedom.

In business, my legacy wasn't money in the bank—it was agents learning integrity. It was showing people that faith and discipline work, even in the marketplace. My real wealth wasn't measured in dollars but in the people I built up, the lives I influenced, and the standards I refused to lower.

In ministry, my legacy wasn't the number of sermons preached—it was souls reached, disciples made, and seeds sown in good soil. I realized the greatest sermon I could ever preach was the one I lived every day. My children, my coworkers, my community—they were all watching my life more closely than they were listening to my words. Proverbs 13:22 says, "A good man leaves an inheritance to his children's children." That's legacy. It flows beyond you. It impacts not just your children, but your grandchildren—and everyone in your line who comes after you.

Here's the truth: we're all leaving a legacy. The question is: what kind?

- Curses or blessings?
- Debt or discipline?
- Excuses or endurance?
- Compromise or conviction?

Legacy isn't optional. You are leaving one whether you mean to or not. Every day you're sowing seeds—your words, your habits, your faith, your integrity. And one day, someone else will eat from what you planted.

So let me challenge you: What story are you writing for the next generation? When your children, your grandchildren, and your great-grandchildren speak your name, what will come to their minds? Will it be excuses? Or will it be excellence? Will it be fear? Or will it be faith?

Living for legacy means living beyond yourself. It means you stop asking, "What do I want right now?" and start asking, "What do I want them to carry later?" Legacy demands sacrifice. Legacy requires discipline. Legacy is built one decision at a time.

Friend, your time on earth is limited, but your legacy is limitless. What you build in faith today can outlive you for generations. So stop settling for survival. Stop living small. Start living for legacy.

Day 20 – Lessons from Leaving a Legacy

- Legacy is not what you leave to people—it's what you leave in them.
- You are always sowing seeds; one day you and others will reap the harvest.
- Every choice builds either curses or blessings for future generations.

Day 20 - Reflection Questions

1. What kind of legacy are you currently building—one of excuses or one of endurance?

_____

_____

_____

2. How do you want your children and grandchildren to remember you?

_____

_____

_____

3. What daily habits right now are shaping your legacy—for better or worse?

_____

_____

_____

Day 20 - No Excuses Challenge

Write down the legacy you want to leave in one sentence.

Example: "I want to leave a legacy of faith, discipline, and love."

Then write down three practical actions you will take this week to start building that legacy.
No excuses—your future generations are depending on you.

Day 21
Eternal Perspective: Living to Honor Jesus

At the end of it all—after the gangs, the jails, the betrayals, the rebuilding, the business, the fitness, the family—I see one thing: Jesus.

He was there in Valley Stream when my family cracked. He was there in Brooklyn when fear walked in. He was there in Puerto Rico when chaos surrounded me. He was there in Spofford when I thought my life was over. He was there in 2005 when I buried my brother and held my child.

He was there when my home burned down and when He gave me back more than I lost. He was there when I rebuilt my life, my family, my business, and my faith. And He is here now.

Everything I've lived, everything I've built, everything I've endured—it's all for one reason: to honor Him. Family is a blessing. Business is a blessing. Fitness is a blessing. Ministry is a blessing. But hear me clearly: all of it is meaningless without Jesus.

Matthew 16:26 says, "What good will it be for someone to gain the whole world, yet forfeit their soul?" The world can hand you money, power, houses, titles, even applause—but none of it matters if your soul is empty.

I live now for one reward: to hear Him say, "Well done, good and faithful servant." That's eternal perspective. That's the finish line worth running toward.

And friend, this is where the "No Excuses" philosophy finds its ultimate home. Because at the end of the day, excuses won't matter. The only thing that matters is faithfulness. Did you live for Him? Did you use your time, your gifts, your influence, to bring Him glory? Did you love well, serve well, endure well?

Your life is a vapor, but eternity is forever. Live today as if eternity is real—because it is.

Day 21 – Lessons from Eternal Perspective: Living to Honor Jesus

- Jesus has been present in every season of your life.
- Earthly success means nothing without eternal purpose.
- The ultimate reward is hearing: "Well done, good and faithful servant.

Day 21 - Reflection Questions

1. Where have you been chasing temporary success instead of eternal purpose?

_____

_____

_____

2. Do you live daily with eternity in mind—or only when life gets hard?

_____

_____

_____

3. What would it look like for you to honor Jesus with every area of your life?

_____

_____

_____

Day 21 – No Excuses Challenge

Write down one area you've been holding back from God. Today, surrender it fully. Say out loud:

"This belongs to You, Lord. I live to honor You."

No excuses—choose eternal over temporary.

Bonus Day 1
My Beginnings

I was born in Valley Stream, New York, into a family that was already divided. My father worked as a Correctional Officer at Rikers Island, walking the tiers and steel corridors of one of the toughest jails in America; my mother was a singer in the Brooklyn Tabernacle Choir, lifting her voice to God every week. My life began with two very different worlds around me —steel bars, prisoners, and authority on one side; music, worship, and the presence of God on the other.

Not long after I was born, my parents separated. That separation set the stage for instability that would follow me for years. My mother took my brother and me to live in Southwest Brooklyn. We were young and unaware, but even as a child, I could feel the weight of our circumstances pressing down on us.

When I was three years old, our Brooklyn home was burglarized. I remember the fear of that moment—not just because of what was stolen, but because the very sense of safety was ripped away. For a child, a home is supposed to be the safest place in the world. That night, I learned that even home could be violated.

In an effort to escape the chaos of the city, my mother decided to move us to Puerto Rico. We settled in Torres De Sabana, one of the island's most notorious housing projects. The stairwells smelled like smoke, and the echo of gunshots—not fireworks—cut through the night. Gangs marked the buildings; drugs were easy to find; poverty wasn't a statistic—it was our daily reality. As a child, you don't fully understand danger, but you feel it. I felt it walking to school, standing outside, and lying in bed while listening for every sound outside, wondering if tonight would be another night something went wrong.

Finances collapsed. We became homeless. Sometimes it was family or friends who took us in; sometimes there simply wasn't a stable place to go. I started to carry a belief that everything could fall apart at any moment—that life itself wasn't secure. The ground under my feet always seemed to shift.

Eventually, addiction took hold of my mother in ways a kid shouldn't have to witness. Out of love and necessity, my grandparents stepped in. They brought my brother and me back to Elmont, Long Island, and their home became our shelter. I was eight years old when I settled there and would remain until I was about twelve. They took us to Saint Boniface Catholic Church in Elmont, and while I learned to appreciate the reverence of tradition, I also carried deep questions and wounds that mass and routine allowed me to hide, not heal.

I went through the motions, but the questions about my life, my mother, and my identity stayed heavy on my chest.

My grandparents provided stability, but they couldn't erase abandonment. I loved my mother. I wanted her. But addiction had stolen her from me. That's a wound that doesn't just heal because you've got a roof and meals on the table.

Around this time, my father re-entered my life in a new way. He had battled alcoholism, been delivered, and completed a Christian men's recovery program. He was now the Assistant Director at New Life For Youth in Beaverdam, Virginia—a residential program where men straight from jail, addiction, and the streets came to recover and rebuild. My brother and I went to live with him at the facility.

It wasn't a normal environment for a kid. We lived among recovering men, hearing their stories and seeing their struggles up close. We attended New Life Outreach International in Richmond, Virginia, every Sunday and Wednesday—mandatory for residents and for us. At first, the church was a culture shock to me. I had come from the quiet reverence of Saint Boniface in Elmont to a lively, Spirit-filled community that believed God still saves, heals, and delivers—right now, not just in theory. Over time, I grew to love the presence of God I felt there, real,alive, and impossible to ignore. It softened parts of me I didn't know had hardened.

I gave my life to Jesus at 13 years old. I joined the Royal Rangers program for youth. I carried my Bible to school and preached to other kids, even when I got mocked for it. I sat in my father's sermons and began to feel a strong pull to speak truth myself.

One day, I asked my father if I could preach to the residents in the program. He said yes. My first sermon was on the Ten Commandments—a 13-year-old kid with a Bible and a burning heart, preaching to men older than me, many of whom had seen more life than most. Men who had faced prison, addiction, loss, violence, and regret. Yet they listened to me with respect, and that changed something inside of me.

But as quickly as I was finding my footing, life shifted again. My father was transferred to the Bronx to pioneer a new branch of the recovery program. We went with him. Not long after, the Fire Marshal shut it down for code violations. With that door closed, my father took night security at the World Trade Center, and we moved into the Allerton Co-Ops on Bronx Park East— notorious projects with the same old pressures I'd known too well: gangs, drugs, survival.

My father remarried. He worked nights. My brother and I were left on our own most evenings. The Bronx pulled on all my old insecurities and anger. He knew where

I started to drift from the faith I had embraced. I began running with the wrong crowd again. I can still remember the moment everything started to tip: my father overheard a conversation between my brother and me, we were talking about being accomplices in a burglary where the house caught fire and burned to the ground.

He knew the streets were tightening their grip. He new where this path led—prison or death. So he did one of the hardest things a father can do: he turned us in.

I was arrested for arson and burglary and sent to Spofford Juvenile Detention Center in the Bronx. Spofford wasn't designed to heal—it was built to contain. From there, I was sentenced to the Midlands Evaluation Center in Columbia, South Carolina, a quasi-military facility for adjudicated youth. That was my first real taste of a structured environment where discipline wasn't optional, where every mistake cost you, and every choice mattered.

Even so, even through all that movement, God had been threading grace through my story: from the grandparents who rescued us to the first sermon I preached, God had a plan.

My beginning wasn't pretty, but it was purposeful, and every moment, good or painful, was shaping the man I was becoming.

Bonus Day 1 Message
Your Beginning Doesn't Get the Last Word

If you grew up under instability, addiction, poverty, or violence, I know what that feels like. If you've changed cities and still carried the same pain with you, I know that, too. If you've watched a parent lose a battle with addiction and asked, "Why wasn't I enough?", I've asked the same question.

But hear me: your beginning is not your ending. The cracks in your early years don't disqualify you—they prepare you. The very instability that tried to break you can become the soil where God plants discipline, faith, and purpose. He can take a childhood like mine—Valley Stream, Brooklyn, Torres De Sabana, Elmont, Beaverdam, the Bronx—and build a man who chooses no excuses.

Don't judge your future by your first chapters. Build anyway. Pray anyway. Get up anyway. God can take the worst parts of your beginning and forge a life that stands when the wind blows. Your beginning doesn't get the last word. You, with God's grace and relentless discipline, do.

Bonus Day 2
My First Downfalls

When I was finally released from Midlands Evaluation Center in Columbia, South Carolina, the court placed me on five years of probation. I reunited with my mother, who had moved to South Carolina to start a new life, because the state wouldn't transfer my probation. It felt like another turn in my story, another unexpected road I had no choice but to walk.

We tried to build something together, but we were struggling financially from the very beginning. Before long, we wound up in the Salvation Army homeless shelter. That shelter became our home for several months. Sleeping in rows of beds, living among strangers who were each carrying their own pain and failures, it was both humbling and humiliating. I was still just a teenager, and yet I felt like I had already lost the battle of life.

Eventually, we found a place at Valley Homes, a low-income housing development in Gloverville, South Carolina. On the outside, it looked like stability. But inside those walls, drugs, crime, and despair lurked at every corner. It wasn't long before I started to slip again. I began violating my probation, pulled into drug abuse and criminal activity. Each violation led to more trouble, and I spent most of my remaining youth shuffling in and out of detention centers and institutions. I had tasted freedom, but I didn't know how to live it without destroying myself.

For years, I went back and forth between South Carolina and New York. Sometimes I lived with family members, other times I was just surviving wherever I could. But no matter the place, the same pain, the same anger, and the same rebellion followed me. It was like a shadow I couldn't shake.

Eventually, the law caught up with me again. I became wanted by the Aiken County Police Department for a gun charge. By early 2000, I felt the walls closing in. I was still so young, but my life was already stacked with probation violations, criminal records, and now a warrant.

So I ran. In 2000, I fled South Carolina and went back to New York, warrant still hanging over me. I went to live with my brother in Jamaica, Queens. He was a member of the Latin Kings gang at the time, and through him, I became affiliated with the gang myself. What I thought would be refuge quickly became another trap.

It wasn't long before I was arrested again—this time for a robbery. The arrest came after a violent clash between the Latin Kings and MS-13, a rival gang, inside a bar in Hempstead, New York. Chaos, violence, pride, and destruction surrounded me, and I was right in the middle of it. That arrest earned me a year in the Nassau County Detention Center.

Looking back, I can see that I had only traded one prison for another. Even when I wasn't behind bars, I was shackled by drugs, by gangs, by my own rebellion. I thought I was living free, but I was in chains the entire time.

Bonus Day 2 Message
Running from Chains Only Finds You New Ones

When I left South Carolina and fled to New York, I thought I was running from chains. In reality, I was just trading one set for another. Probation, drugs, detention centers, the shelter—all of it was already prison. And when I joined the Latin Kings, I only added more chains to my life.

This is what I've learned: if you don't let God break your chains, you'll only keep switching them out. A new city, a new gang, a new hustle—it all feels different for a moment, but it's still bondage.

I thought freedom meant doing whatever I wanted. But real freedom isn't found in rebellion—it's found in discipline, in surrender, in purpose. And until I chose that, I was just running in circles, adding scars, adding time, adding regrets. Don't let the streets lie to you.

Don't let rebellion trick you into thinking you're free. I was there, I lived it, and I can tell you: every step away from God is another chain. Real freedom comes when you stop running and let Him break the cycle once and for all.

Bonus Day 3
Running & Wandering

While I was incarcerated, I couldn't seem to keep myself from trouble. I was filled with anger—angry at the system, angry at my family, angry at God, and most of all, angry at myself. That anger exploded over and over again, and because of it, I was separated from the rest of the inmates. I ended up serving six months of my sentence in solitary confinement, locked in a cell alone, because I couldn't control my temper. I lashed out at correctional officers. I fought with other inmates. I carried a rage that burned like fire, and the system's answer was to put me in isolation.

It broke me and hardened me at the same time. In the silence of solitary, there was nowhere to run from myself. The walls pressed in, and I was forced to confront who I was becoming. But even there, in that broken place, there was a spark of light. Somehow, I managed to channel my energy into finishing school. Against all odds, I worked through my studies, and when I took the GED test, I scored some of the highest grades in science, math, and writing. For the first time in a long time, I felt hope. I thought maybe, just maybe, i wasn't as lost as I had believed.

I began dreaming again. I told myself that when I got out, I would attend college. I wanted to major in psychology, maybe help others like me who had gone through trauma and anger. For a moment, I believed that when the doors opened, I'd walk into a new life.

But life had other plans. When my sentence ended, I wasn't set free. Instead, I was extradited back to South Carolina to face a warrant that had been issued while I was locked up. I was convicted of presenting a firearm at a person, and just like that, I was sentenced again—more time, more probation, more chains. My hopes of college and a new life felt like they were slipping through my hands.

When I was released again, I tried once more to rebuild. I moved to Jacksonville, Florida, to live with my Aunt Nilka and Uncle Gilbert. They gave me shelter, and for a little while, I believed I had a chance. I thought about joining the military. I thought about going to college. I wanted to prove to my family—and to myself—that I could be more than the kid with a record.

But temptation came knocking again. I got arrested on a burglary charge, and instead of facing it, I panicked. I jumped bail, knowing it would mean another probation violation. Another warrant was issued for my arrest. Rather than dealing with it, I ran. I fled to Miami, Florida, trying to disappear, trying to escape the cycle.

By this time, I had lost almost all hope that I'd ever escape the criminal lifestyle. With the warrant hanging over me, I figured my future was already ruined. So I turned back to what I knew— I started selling marijuana. I lived out of hotels and hostels in South Beach, scraping together enough to cover a night here or there. When I couldn't make enough, I was homeless, sleeping on the streets of Miami. Homelessness stripped me bare. The streets were unforgiving, and every night I felt the weight of shame pressing down on me like tonne of bricks I couldn't push off.

Then came an encounter that would change the direction of my life, at least for a season. One night at a Miami club, I sold marijuana to a salesman named "Dredd" who was on vacation. He wasn't just impressed with the weed—he was impressed with my sales tactics. He saw something in me I didn't see in myself. He offered me a job with a place to stay. Desperate to get off the streets, I took the offer and joined Chapel Sales, a door-to-door magazine sales company.

For the next several months, I traveled all over Florida, knocking on doors, selling magazines. It wasn't glamorous, but for the first time in years, I had consistency. Dredd became a mentor to me. He taught me how to sell, how to approach people, how to turn rejection into resilience. Looking back, that's where I first learned the skills that would one day shape my future in business. God was planting seeds even when I didn't realize it.

But trouble still had my name. While selling magazines door-to-door, I ended up in St. Cloud, Florida. I didn't know the city had a law against soliciting. One homeowner called the police on me, and when they ran my name, my warrant came up. They cited me for unlicensed soliciting, and when they searched me, they found marijuana in my pocket.

I was arrested on the spot and charged with petty possession of marijuana. They sent me to the Osceola County Correctional Facility in Kissimmee, Florida. I thought it would be a short stay, but instead, it was another step deeper into the system. From there, I was extradited to Clay County Jail to face my outstanding warrant.

The sentences stacked up. In Osceola County, I got one year of probation for the marijuana charge. Then in Clay County, I was sentenced to six months in jail for the burglary warrant and for violating probation.

But here's where everything began to shift. In Osceola County Correctional Facility, I hit the lowest point yet—and found myself reaching upward. It was there that I re-dedicated my life to Jesus Christ. I picked up the Bible again, and I couldn't stop reading it. I started preaching inside those walls, becoming a "jail preacher" to other inmates. The very place meant to break me became the place where my faith came alive again.

When I was later extradited to Clay County Jail, I carried that fire with me. Even though I was serving another six months, this time it was different. I wasn't just another inmate. I was a man of God rediscovering his calling, even behind bars.

Bonus Day 3 Message
God Can Meet You in a Jail Cell

I spent six months in solitary, convinced that anger owned me. I thought violence and rebellion were all I had left. But even in solitary, God had a plan. He let me finish my education. He let me taste hope. And when I thought I was done, when I thought the system had swallowed me whole, He stepped in again.

It was in jail—in the very place meant to cage me—that I found freedom. I picked up a Bible, and the words leapt off the page. I started preaching to men who, like me, thought their lives were over. But God reminded me: no place is too dark for Him to shine His light.

Maybe you feel trapped right now. Maybe you're in your own kind of prison—an addiction, a relationship, a past mistake. Hear me: God can meet you there. He doesn't wait until you're out and polished. He'll come to you in your brokenness, in your mess, in your cell. And when He shows up, chains break.

I was once a prisoner, but inside those walls, I discovered the freedom of Christ. And that's why I say it without apology: God can meet you in a jail cell—and if He can free me there, He can free you anywhere.

Bonus Day 4
Broken but Stirred

After my release from Clay County Jail in 2003, I moved to St. Cloud, Florida to complete the remainder of my probation for the marijuana charge. For the first time in years, there was a sense of family restoration. My brother had just been released from prison on parole, and in an effort to reunite us all, my grandfather bought a house for my brother, my mother, and me in St. Cloud. It felt like a new chapter—one where maybe, just maybe, we could piece back together what life had torn apart.

I carried hopes bigger than the mistakes of my past. I wanted to pursue a college degree and carve out a career that my family could finally be proud of. I dreamed of being more than just the kid with a record—I wanted to be proof that change was possible. But not everyone agreed with that path. My grandfather disapproved of college. He insisted that instead of chasing degrees, I should focus on helping my mother with the bills.

So I set aside my college dreams for the moment and focused on survival. I found work as a cook at a local restaurant in St. Cloud. The work was humble, but it gave me a routine—a stability I hadn't known in years. It was there that another piece of my story unfolded. I reconnected with a girl I had met previously in Jacksonville, and she soon landed a job at the same restaurant. We began dating, and for the first time, I thought I could build a future not just for myself, but for us.

While working at the restaurant, she crossed paths with a man who would become very important in my journey—Guillermo Montanez. Guillermo was an ex-Latin King from the Chicago branch, a man who had walked a path like mine but had chosen a different ending. She introduced us, and Guillermo extended an invitation that would shape the next stage of my life: an invitation to church.

The church was called Freedom Tabernacle (now known as Freedom Life Church) in Kissimmee, Florida. That invitation turned into transformation. We became members, and I enrolled at Freedom Bible College to deepen my walk with God. My faith wasn't just about jailhouse prayers anymore—it was becoming a lifestyle.

Outside of church, Guillermo gave me a chance to work with him in construction. The job gave me income, but more than that, it gave me mentorship. I wasn't just building houses—I was slowly learning to rebuild my life.

Wanting to settle down, I began searching for a place to live with my girlfriend. We eventually found a mobile home for rent near my job. But there was a conviction in my heart. I didn't want to live in sin, cohabiting outside of marriage. So we made a decision: if we were going to live together, it would be as husband and wife.

In 2005, we got married, and not long after, she became pregnant with our first child. It was a moment of joy, of hope, of finally beginning to build a family of my own.

My brother David attended the wedding. He was excited for me. I could see it in his eyes—he wanted what I was finding. He wanted change, but he didn't know how to let go of the streets. David continued clinging to the criminal lifestyle he had known even before prison. Yet Guillermo and I never stopped inviting him to church.

And he came. He showed up a few times, and on one of those days, Guillermo had the privilege of leading my brother David to Jesus in prayer. I'll never forget the moment—it was proof that God could reach anyone, even the ones you thought were too far gone.

But salvation doesn't erase struggle overnight. David wrestled to let go of the street life. And then came the tragedy I'll never forget. On April 27, 2005, David suffered an accidental gunshot wound to the leg. The bullet severed a major artery in his thigh, and my brother bled out and died. I was crushed. My brother was gone. Just as hope was starting

to take root in my life, death knocked on our family's door again. But even in the grief, I clung to one thing: David had called on Jesus before he left this earth. And I trust that even in his last moments, God's mercy held him.

Bonus Day 4 Message
Hold On to Hope, Even in Loss

The hardest thing I've ever lived through was watching my brother die just as he was tasting freedom. I wanted him to have the life I was starting to find—the stability, the faith, the family. And for a while, it seemed like maybe he would. But then, in one tragic moment, it was gone.

Here's what I learned: even when life rips someone from you, even when the pain is unbearable, hope remains. David called on the name of Jesus before he died. That means I will see my brother again. Death had the last word over his body, but not over his soul.

If you've lost someone, don't let despair write the ending. Hold on to the hope that God offers. His mercy reaches farther than our mistakes. His grace is stronger than the streets. And His love doesn't let go, even in death.

My brother's story is part of my story. His loss fuels my mission: to help others choose life before it's too late. I live with pain, yes—but I also live with purpose. And I refuse to waste the second chance God has given me.

Bonus Day 5
Survival Hustle

After my brother David died, I fell into a deep depression. It felt like a hole had opened beneath me, and I was freefalling with no bottom in sight. Losing him broke something inside me that I wasn't sure could ever be repaired. But even in my grief, I refused to let go of my faith. I kept going to church. I kept pressing into Jesus. My heart was shattered, but my hands stayed lifted.

Looking back, I can honestly say that 2005 was both the worst and the best year of my life. The worst, because I buried my brother. The best, because in the same year, God gave me a gift that kept me moving forward: the birth of my first son that September. Holding that baby boy in my arms for the first time, I realized that God wasn't done with me. He had taken something precious, but He had also placed a new responsibility, a new purpose, and a new legacy in my hands. A year later, in October 2006, my second son was born. I was a father of two, and with all my flaws and all my failures, I was determined to give them a better life. But life wasn't done testing me. My first marriage eventually ended in divorce.

Suddenly, I was left standing as a single father to two little boys. The weight of it was crushing at times. I didn't just have to take care of myself anymore—I had to be the provider, the protector, and the example for them.

By 2007, I made a decision. I wanted stability, benefits, a steady income, and a way to provide for my sons. I decided to join the military. I studied hard, took the Armed Services Vocational Aptitude Battery test (ASVAB), and scored extremely high. For a moment, I thought this was the door God had opened. But then the past came back to haunt me. My felony record blocked me from the Military Occupational Specialty (MOS) I wanted. The only thing they offered me was Infantry.

I didn't want to settle. Something in me knew I wasn't supposed to spend my life simply following orders with a rifle in my hands. So I turned toward another dream: college. I wanted to study psychology, to learn how the mind worked, to understand pain and trauma—not just mine, but everyone's. I wanted to help people climb out of the same holes I had fallen into.

In 2008, I applied to Valencia College and was accepted. But the road wasn't easy. With no financial aid, I worked two jobs just to keep up with tuition, bills, and taking care of my boys. Every dollar I earned had a destination, and every day was a battle to keep going.

But I wanted more than just survival. I wanted to build something lasting. Music had always been in my blood since childhood, so I decided to take a risk. I opened a recording studio inside a small local thrift shop. I called it J. Box Recordings.

That studio became my second home. Long nights, endless hours—I sold beats, produced tracks, edited music for up-and-coming artists, and even performed at local shows. For a while, it felt like a dream in motion. I wasn't just making money—I was creating, inspiring, and chasing something I had always loved.

But the financial weight was heavier than my shoulders could carry. Business is hard when all you have is grit but no capital. Eventually, I couldn't keep up. J. Box Recordings closed its doors. Another dream cut short. Another lesson in the school of hard knocks.

With no choice, I went back to working regular jobs. I landed a position in construction with a concrete company called Prestige A & B Ready Mix. My work ethic spoke for itself, and before long, I was promoted to concrete repair manager. While there, I also earned my CDL license. It wasn't glamorous, but it was honest work, and it kept food on the table for my boys. Looking back, I realize those years were survival years. They were about keeping my sons clothed, fed, and safe while I was still trying to figure out who I was. It was a hustle, yes—but it was also a season of proving to myself that I could keep standing no matter how many times life tried to knock me down.

Bonus Day 5 Message
Survival is Not the End—It's Training Ground

When my marriage ended, when I was left with two sons and no clear direction, I thought survival was all I had left. Work, hustle, grind, repeat. Two jobs, late nights, running on fumes. I thought I was stuck in survival forever.

But here's what I learned: survival seasons are training seasons. God doesn't waste your grind. Every long night at J. Box Recordings, every early morning at the concrete company, every dollar I fought for—it was preparing me for more. It taught me responsibility. It taught me discipline. It taught me that excuses don't feed children and laziness doesn't build legacies.

Maybe you're in your survival season right now. It feels like you're just getting by, like all you're doing is working to keep the lights on. Don't despise it. Use it. Let it sharpen you. Let it mold you. Survival is not your final destination—it's the gym where God trains you for the life you're really called to live.

I survived. And because I survived, I learned how to thrive. And so can you.

Bonus Day 6
Jail Redemption

One day, while fixing a pool at a mansion in Windermere, Florida, my life took another unexpected turn. The house belonged to Michael, a venture capitalist from New York. I was there to do a job, but Michael and his wife noticed something more than just the work I was doing. They saw my work ethic.

When I finished the job, they invited me to lunch. At first, I thought it was just a courtesy. But as we sat down together, that lunch became something I now call my introduction to the entrepreneurial spirit.

Over plates of food and casual conversation, I asked them a question that had been stirring in me for years: "What does it take to be successful in business?" Michael's answer was simple: "Work hard and save money." It was good advice, but his wife added something that hit me differently. She looked me in the eye and told me to read three books:

1. Rich Dad, Poor Dad by Robert Kiyosaki
2. Think and Grow Rich by Napoleon Hill
3. How to Win Friends & Influence People by Dale Carnegie

I remember nodding politely, but in my heart I thought, How are three books supposed to change my financial situation? I was drowning in responsibilities, trying to raise two boys as a single father. Books didn't seem like the answer. Still, their words stuck with me.

Something about that lunch awakened a fire in me. I realized I had always had an entrepreneurial spirit—a hunger to build, to create, to take risks. So, I decided to "try my luck." I took my savings and opened a home recording studio and a tattoo business, hoping that this time, I could make it work.

But dreams without capital are fragile. The truth is, I didn't have enough start-up money, and I made poor financial choices. The businesses failed. I had to shut them down. Another set of doors closed. Another reminder that wanting something badly isn't enough—you have to prepare, plan, and sacrifice to make it real.

Yet even in those failures, I learned. I call them trials and errors. Every failed business taught me that there's more to ownership than desire. To succeed would mean more hours, more discipline, more risk—and the hardest truth of all: less time with my children. That tension never left me.

But life had another gift waiting for me.

In 2009, I reconnected with someone who had once held my heart—Brenda. She was my high school sweetheart, the girl I first dated at 15 years old when I lived with my grandparents in New York. Years had passed, but one day, while scrolling Myspace, I found her again. We started talking over the phone, and little by little, the old connection came alive.

Our conversations grew longer. We laughed, we remembered, and soon we became close again. Eventually, she moved to Florida and started working at the University of Central Florida, serving as a secretary for the business incubator. It was almost poetic: while I was chasing business lessons through failures, she was working in an environment designed to nurture entrepreneurs.

She started attending the same church I did and lived with an elderly couple who were members there. Over time, we began courting seriously in 2010. My sons adored her, and she loved them like her own.

In 2011, Brenda and I got married. That year, I didn't just gain a wife—I gained a partner who believed in me, stood by me, and chose to adopt my two children as her own.

After years of loss, failure, and struggle, God gave me a new chapter of restoration.

Bonus Day 6 Message
Failure is a Teacher, Not a Death Sentence

I can't count how many times I've failed. Businesses collapsed. Dreams went bankrupt. Plans fell apart. And every time, I thought, This is the end. But now I know—it was never the end. It was the classroom.

Failure taught me discipline. It taught me humility. It taught me that vision without preparation is just fantasy. And most importantly, it taught me that even in my lowest moments, God was still writing my story.

And then came Brenda. After years of heartbreak, God brought me someone who believed in me when I barely believed in myself. Someone who didn't just marry me but chose to adopt my children and build a family with me.

Listen: your failures do not disqualify you. They prepare you. They break pride, sharpen faith, and shape character. Don't fear failure—fear giving up. Because on the other side of every collapse, there's another chance. And if you keep standing, God will send the right people and open the right doors.

I learned that failure wasn't my enemy—it was my training

ground. And with God, even broken beginnings can lead to beautiful restorations.

Bonus Day 7
Family & Legacy

With the unwavering support of my wife, I finally took the advice Michael and his wife had given me years before—I started to read. Not just casually, not just flipping pages—I devoured those books. Rich Dad, Poor Dad, Think and Grow Rich, and How to Win Friends & Influence People weren't just books; they became keys that unlocked my mindset. They challenged me to think differently about money, discipline, and influence.

Those books lit a fire inside me. I began attending business networking events, showing up in rooms where people were smarter, wealthier, and further along than me. I listened, I learned, and I asked questions. Soon, reading became my habit, my discipline, and my edge. I set a goal: 25 to 50 self-help and business finance books every year. Page after page, I was feeding my mind what it needed to grow into the man I wanted to become.

With prayer, support, and relentless work, I finally opened my first successful business: We ROC Construction LLC. My good friend Guillermo, who had once invited me to church and stood by me through some of the hardest years of my life, also started his own business, GM Master Painting LLC. Together, we were building something bigger than jobs—we were building legacies.

In 2012, my path crossed into a new industry: real estate. While working as a remodeling contractor for my own business, I landed several large contracts with hotels and investors. The money started coming in, and for the first time, I saw the possibility of ownership. I began saving, and with the help of a $20,000 loan from my grandfather, I purchased my first investment property.

I planned to flip it for a profit. To save on commissions, I set out to get my real estate license. But it wasn't easy. I failed the exam once, twice, three times. By the sixth attempt, frustration weighed heavy. But I refused to give up. On the seventh try, I passed. That moment became a symbol for my life: I may fail, but I won't quit.

Then life hit me hard again. My family's home burned down, and to make it worse, my insurance company—Security First— denied the claim. With no home, I had to move my family into my investment property. My dream flip had now become our shelter.

The remodel drained my finances. I ran out of capital and didn't even have enough to join the National Association of Realtors (NAR), which my broker required. Because of that, I couldn't fully practice in the field the way I had planned.

With bills mounting, I took a seasonal job in timeshare sales, since NAR membership wasn't required. I walked into that role reluctantly, but quickly realized something powerful: I had always had a gift for sales. It was in my DNA. Before long, I wasn't just selling—I was thriving.

While still building my construction business, I hit my stride in sales. At Westgate Resorts, I was promoted to T.O. Manager (management-level closer). Hungry to grow, I took additional sales courses and was eventually recruited as a sales trainer. I became obsessed with learning the psychology of sales and mastering the art of recruiting new agents.

By 2016, I had sold over $1,000,000 in timeshare and was honored as Sales Trainer of the Year at Westgate's annual sales convention in Kissimmee, Florida.

That success gave me the courage to take the next leap. I sold my first business, stepped away from timeshare, and launched my own real estate company: Gines Investment Group LLC. We focused on serving investors, teaching them strategies that I had once struggled to figure out on my own.

From there, the vision expanded. I opened RE Property Services LLC, a traditional residential brokerage, and later launched RePros Agent Academy, an online real estate school to equip and train new agents.

But my purpose didn't stop at business. I never forgot where God found me. I went back to the same place that had changed my life years before: the Osceola County Correctional Facility. Today, I serve as a jail minister, preaching to inmates, showing them that the same God who restored me can restore them too.

My grandparents always told me: "If you want something great in life, you'll have to work hard for it." I've lived through loss, addiction, poverty, rejection, and failure—but I've also lived through restoration, discipline, faith, and breakthrough. That work ethic has carried me through every trauma and every trial, and today I use it to serve both my agents and clients, helping them reach their goals.

Now, I live in Central Florida with my beautiful wife and our five children. I love spending time with my family, building a future for them, and pouring into my community. I am proud to stand not just as a businessman, but as a father, husband, servant, and man of God—proof that no excuses can stand in the way of God's plan when you surrender your life to Him.

Bonus Day 7 Message
Build a Legacy That Outlives You

When I look at my life, I see failure, pain, and brokenness. But I also see discipline, restoration, and growth. I see how God used every tragedy as training and every setback as a setup. I see how faith, family, and relentless work created a legacy I can now pass to my children.

That's what this journey is about—not just surviving, not just hustling, but building something that lasts beyond you. Money comes and goes. Businesses succeed and fail. But legacy—what you leave in people, in your children, in your community—that's eternal.

You don't have to come from wealth to leave wealth. You don't have to be born into success to build success. All you need is faith, discipline, and the courage to keep going when failure tells you to quit.

I built my legacy brick by brick—sometimes with tears in my eyes, sometimes with nothing in my pockets, but always with hope in my heart. And if I can, so can you.

Your story isn't over. In fact, the best chapters may still be ahead. Don't just aim to live—aim to leave a legacy that points

to God, inspires discipline, and shows the next generation
what's possible

About the Author

Jesse S. Gines is a speaker, entrepreneur, chaplain, and motivator whose life embodies transformation through discipline, faith, and personal responsibility. Rising from a childhood marked by instability, poverty, and adversity, Jesse rebuilt his life through relentless dedication and an unwavering commitment to growth. His story reflects the reality that change is not an accident, it is a decision backed by consistent action.

As a businessman and real estate broker/investor, Jesse has built a career grounded in integrity and hard work. As a minister and inspirational voice, he is dedicated to reaching people from every walk of life, those fighting through struggle, pursuing purpose, or seeking a deeper understanding of themselves.

Jesse's message is anchored in a simple but uncompromising principle: **No Excuses**. He challenges readers and audiences alike to reject limitations, confront their pain, and cultivate a life rooted in purpose and accountability. Through his books, teachings, and public speaking, Jesse aims to inspire breakthrough.

His work blends practical wisdom, faith-based principles, and real-world experience, offering a clear path for people who are ready to rise above their past and build a future worthy of their potential.

Jesse lives by the belief that every life has a calling, every struggle carries a meaning, and and every person, regardless of where they begin, can rewrite their story with courage, discipline, and conviction.